Mac and Cheese: Quick and Easy Comfort

Gina Lynn

ʃynchron8
Ↄ Publishing

Synchron8 Publishing
www.synchron8publishing.com

ISBN Number: 978-1-942535-00-3 (eBook)

ISBN Number: 978-1-942535-01-0 (Paperback)

THANK YOU!

While I love all types of foods, drinks and cooking experiences, my biggest goal is to provide readers with creative and satisfying recipes in a way that is valuable to them. I recognize that there are a variety of options for finding dinner and other meal ideas, and I appreciate the fact that you have decided to purchase this book. As an added thank you, I am offering a free gift to you, my readers. With this book, you can receive an additional collection of delish mac and cheese recipes that are not included here. They are just as tasty as the ones featured in this book (though some may argue the extras are even better). It is simply a way of saying thank you for your support.

To get the collection of free mac and cheese recipes, visit:

www.synchron8publishing.com/GLMacandCheese

I hope you enjoy the cheesy goodness ahead. When you are done, don't forget to leave a review for others who might benefit from the book. It doesn't take much, even if it's just a note on which recipe is your new favorite. It is much appreciated, and once again, thank you.

Table of Contents

8 OPTIONS TO PUMP UP THE PARMA-ALFREDO MAC AND CHEESE 45

8 EAT'EM UP, NO-BAKE YELLOW MAC AND CHEESE OPTIONS 63

10 TOP THICK AND CREAMY CUSTARD-STYLE MAC AND CHEESE OPTIONS 81

CONCLUSION 103

ABOUT SYNCHRON8 PUBLISHING 104

Introduction

There are certain foods that can provide a reason to smile no matter what the day has brought your way. Mac and cheese is one of those quintessential dishes. It doesn't matter whether the dish is simple and presented to a youngster to suit the child's palate or as a decadent dish for a discerning connoisseur, mac and cheese brings the joy out in all forms of dining experiences.

What if you could have a quick and easy dish that could please young and old alike?

What if you could have dozens of options for turning an easy and quick dish into a more satisfying meal?

What if you could have true homemade goodness in about the same time it takes to make the budget boxed stuff?

What if you could create mac and cheese dishes that reflect your food favorites from around the globe?

You can! With these 40 mac and cheese recipes you can address all of these questions with a resounding cheer from cheesy enjoyment from those you serve. Forget those budget boxes of noodles and powered cheese forever! Once you start to explore the options that you have within the world of mac and cheese, you'll never go back to the cheap and unsatisfying stuff ever again.

I have a simple mac and cheese system that can lead to nearly unlimited possibilities. All you need to do is understand 4 basic recipes that serve as the bases for your dishes. You can enjoy baked goodness, or stuck to the stove top with both quick and easy as extra creamy bases. Once to master the base recipes, you can customize and experiment with your favorite flavors and ingredients to make the options in this book or create cheesy comfort of your own. All of the bases take less than 30 minutes (including the baked ones). In fact many of the recipes in this book can be completed in about half that time, making a perfect side dish or quick and easy weeknight meal.

A Note about Cheeses

Before we begin to explore the actual mac and cheese recipes, there is some important information you need to know about the nature of cheeses. Not every cheese is created equal, and not every cheese will work for successful mac and cheese.

The recipes in this book serve not only as a guide to creamy, rich, satisfying goodness, but my goal is also to inspire you to use your own culinary creativity to create dishes that you enjoy.

Before you experiment with the recipes and seek to change out some of the cheeses noted in recipes, whether due to personal preference or experimentation, there are some points about certain cheeses that you should know.

Hard Cheeses: You will want to avoid using hard cheeses such as Swiss cheese in the actual mac and cheese dish. Hard cheeses do not melt well. If your love of these cheeses calls out their use in your creations, they are best used as a topping or garnish over the top of a finished dished.

Bleu Cheese: I personally love the bold taste of Bleu Cheese. While it does melt well in dishes, you need to be aware that the cheese will develop a green color if used in mac and cheese. It is not a sign of spoilage. It is simply a chemical reaction that occurs. I haven't noticed a taste difference, but a green color to your pasta dish can be alarming if you aren't prepared to see it.

Processed Cheese: The recipes for the No Bake Yellow Mac and Cheese (Stove Top Version) require the use of processed cheese. There are a variety of brands on the market. To ensure the most successful incorporation of processed cheese into the dish, add cheese in cubes (approximately a quarter to a half inch). The easiest method for cutting the cheese from a block into cubes is to be sure to cut from the block when it is cold. Have a sharp knife and a cup of hot water while cutting. Dip the knife into the hot water before cutting to avoid having difficulty getting the knife through or having the cheese stick to the knife.

Substituting Cheeses: The recipes in this book were designed to provide consistent and tasty results using fairly typical cheese selections. If you desire to substitute cheeses in dishes, you should be sure to keep the proportions both the overall amount of cheese as well as each type of cheese consistent in your experimentation. For example, a recipe calls for 2 ½ cups of white cheddar and 1 ½ cups of Gruyere, but you want to try Havarti and Fontina instead. Substitute the cheddar with Havarti and Fontina for the Gruyere. (Note: other good substitutions for Gruyere are Provolone and Gouda.)

A Note about Pasta Choices

The choice of pasta used for mac and cheese is not limited to the traditionally accepted elbows from the boxed fare or shells for the creamier style dish. However, there are various reasons for the popularity of these noodles for the respective dishes. While you are always welcome to experiment, after all, your cooking is your cooking, there are some generally followed practices for pasta selection.

Most preferred: Tubular Shapes

The most popular is, of course, elbow macaroni (hence "Mac" and Cheese). Similar choices include penne, rigatoni, and ziti.

The tubes, straight or curved, have blunt cut or slanted ends that catch the cheese sauce nicely. It is important to really stir cheese sauce and noodles together before serving or baking to get the tubes filled. If you use tube pasta that has ridges on the outside, it helps even more cheese cling to the noodle.

Quirky Alternatives: Corkscrews

Options include rotini, fusilli, and cavatappi. For kids, cavatappi is a fun choice as one of the other names it goes by is "scoobi doo". Given that corkscrews have large surface areas for the length of their shapes, the cheese sauce can cling well to the noodle. The difference in the presentation of corkscrews compared to tubes can give standard favorites a new look that is both adult and kid friendly.

More Kid-Friendly Pick-Me-Ups: Shapes

Make meal time fun for young and old alike by using shapes such as shells and bowties. Bell-shaped campanelle is a fresh alternative. Rotelle, with a wheel shape, and radiator, which look like an opened corkscrew/radiator are kid favorites as well.

All of the rough shapes allow cheese to cling to the noodle, though in some cases the rotelle can lose shape during cooking.

Powered Up Options: Stuffed Pastas

To add an additional element of taste and texture to mac and cheese, you can substitute all or part of the pasta in a given dish with pastas such as ravioli or tortellini. The stuffing in the pastas can supplement a basic mac and cheese recipe or even serve to replace some ingredients in different versions. For example, substitute seafood ravioli in the lobster mac and cheese recipe for a quicker prep time or add some meat to the vegetable based recipes with a ground meat tortellini.

A Note about Serving Sizes

Generally speaking, the serving sizes for these dishes are as follows:

- The base recipes, alone, are the equivalent of 1 to 1.5 servings. The overall servings of the recipe are enough to serve one person as under the heading of "a generous portion."
- For the additional options, the servings listed in the recipes are enough to serve 1 to 2 people.
- The recipes have been optimized for "ideal" results but can be halved or doubled, etc. to create dishes, but there may be variations and adjustments to be made in cooking times as a result. The most common differences in cooking/baking times are due to using a bigger or smaller dish than the dimensions noted in the recipes. For smaller dishes, cook times will be reduced and the opposite is true for larger dishes.

Four Mac and Cheese Base Recipes

The mac and cheese recipes in this book are easy to master and tailor to your individual tastes and preferences. The foundations of all the recipes contained in this book can be traced back to four basic mac and cheese bases. The first is a white cheese mac and cheese that is baked. The remaining three are based on a stove top preparation and include an additional white cheese base as well as two yellow cheese options.

The basic mac and cheese recipes can be enjoyed as stand-alone dishes or through a variety of options that are covered later in the book to help jazz up the familiar stand by. Convenience and comfort can combine in these quick and easy dishes. All of the base recipes can be made in less than 30 minutes. In some cases, they can be put together in 15 minutes or less. Plus, recipe options further into the book serve the full range of mac and cheese connoisseur, from the feisty toddler to the refined adult.

Old World Comfort Baked Mac and Cheese
(White Cheese Base)

This is the single, baking required, mac and cheese in this book. While youngsters tend to love the easy and quick stove top versions of mac and cheese, there is something gratifying and extra appealing about the taste from a backed mac and cheese that makes the extra 15 minutes or so worth the wait.

Ingredients and Supplies
Pot of salted boiling water (Kosher salt works best)
Large saucepan
Large (2 quart) baking dish
Mixing bowl for cheeses

8 ounces of pasta (Fusilli or Elbows)
4 tablespoons of unsalted butter
Additional teaspoon of salt
Non-stick spray or additional butter for baking dish
¼ cup all-purpose flour
2 cups of whole milk, warmed
Pinch of Nutmeg
1 bay leaf
2 ½ cups of sharp white cheddar (Keep ½ cup separate to top the dish)
1 ½ cups of Gruyere cheese

Directions
Preheat oven to 400 degrees.
Bring salted water to a boil.

Add pasta and cook until al dente, or slightly undercooked (it will finish while baking or broiling).

While pasta is cooking, melt 4 tablespoons of butter and whisk in flour over medium heat. After whisking flour for two minutes to create a paste, slowly whisk in the warmed milk. Add salt, nutmeg and bay leaf to the mix and whisk intermittently for 8 minutes. In a bowl, Combine 2 cups of white cheddar with the Gruyere and set aside.

Drain pasta, leaving approximately 1 cup of water in with the pasta. This liquid will help the pasta to cook and thicken the final sauce.

Return to the saucepan, remove and discard the bay leaf. Add the blended cheeses to the saucepan. Combine the pasta, liquid and sauce by stirring. The mixture will be a loose consistency that will thicken up while baking.

Coat the baking dish with non-stick spray, butter, or vegetable oil. Pour the mixture into the dish and even the contents out across the dish. Top with the remaining cheddar cheese.

Bake for 15 minutes.

Parma-Alfredo No-Bake Mac and Cheese

(White Cheese Base)

For a quicker version of white cheese mac and cheese, the Parma-Alfredo no-bake provides creamy basic mac and cheese that can go straight from your stove top to your dinner plate.

Ingredients and Supplies
Pot of salted boiling water (Kosher salt works best)
Large skillet

8 ounces of pasta (Penne or other small pasta)
1 garlic clove
1 tablespoon unsalted butter
2 cups heavy cream
1/2 cup shredded Parmigiano-Reggiano (Parmesan) cheese for sauce
1/4 cup of Parmigiano-Reggiano (Parmesan) cheese for topping
1 teaspoon of salt and pepper, plus more to taste

Directions
Bring salted water to a boil.
Add pasta and cook until al dente.
Reserve 1 cup of pasta liquid for sauce.
Drain pasta.

Smash the garlic clove on a cutting board with the side of a large Chef's knife. Rub the skillet with the garlic and toss the clove. Heat the skillet over medium heat and melt the butter. Add the heavy cream and salt and pepper (approximately one teaspoon). Reduce to a low heat and let simmer about 5 minutes until the mixture reduces by about 30%. Stir in ½ cup of Parmigiano-Reggiano followed by the pasta. Add some of the reserved pasta liquid to thicken sauce and stir until sauce is creamy and cheese is melted.

Plate and season with salt and pepper to taste and top with additional cheese.

New World Comfort No-Baked Mac and Cheese

(Yellow Cheese Base)

With the New World No-Bake Mac and Cheese, you can forever ditch the boxed and powdered versions that you grew up knowing. This recipe provides the same level of comfort for about the same amount of time and effort, yet the flavor difference is one that will have people of all ages asking for more.

Ingredients and Supplies
Pot of salted boiling water (Kosher salt works best)
Medium saucepan

8 ounces of pasta (Elbows or Fusilli)
1 tablespoon of unsalted butter
1 tablespoon all-purpose flour
1 teaspoon mustard powder
Cayenne pepper or hot sauce to taste (optional)
12 oz. evaporated milk
1 ½ cups grated yellow cheddar cheese (mild is most universal, but medium, sharp or smoked can add a depth of flavor)
¼ cup cubed processed cheese
Salt and pepper to taste

Directions
Bring salted water to a boil.
Add pasta and cook until al dente.
Reserve 1 cup of pasta liquid for sauce.
Drain pasta.

In the saucepan, melt butter. Over medium heat, whisk in flour, mustard powder, and cayenne or hot sauce. Whisk for 1 minute before slowly incorporating evaporated milk and whisk to thoroughly mix. Lower heat to a simmer and whisk intermittently for about 5 minutes as sauce begins to thicken. Stir in both cheeses. Add enough reserved pasta liquid to further thicken the sauce.

Plate the mac and cheese. Season with salt and pepper to taste.

Thick and Creamy No-Bake Mac and Cheese

(Thicker, Egg Custard Version of the Yellow Cheese Base)

To get and even richer and creamier experience from your mac and cheese, this version of stove top mac and cheese is the ticket. By creating more of a custard base within the mac and cheese, the overall dish provides a deeper flavor with even more stick-to-your-ribs goodness while maintaining stove top to dinner plate ease.

Ingredients and Supplies
Pot of salted boiling water (Kosher salt works best)
Large saucepan

8 ounces of pasta (shells or other small pasta)
½ teaspoon salt
3 tablespoons unsalted butter
2 large eggs
1 cup evaporated milk
3 cups shredded yellow cheddar cheese (Mild is the most universal but medium, sharp, or smoked can be incorporated for a deeper flavor profile)
Pinch of cayenne pepper (optional)

Directions
Bring salted water to a boil.
Add pasta and cook until al dente.
Reserve 1 cup of pasta liquid for sauce.
Drain pasta.
Toss in butter until melted and coating pasta.

In large saucepan over medium heat, whisk eggs, evaporated milk, salt, cheese, and cayenne pepper together. Continue to whisk until the mixture thickens (approximately 3 minutes). Add pasta and continue to stir and cook for another 2-3 minutes. Add reserved pasta liquid to thicken the sauce while stirring.

Plate and season with additional salt and pepper to taste.

10 Flavorful Options for the Old World Mac and Cheese

Here is where we begin to take the basic mac and cheese recipes up a notch. Some of the variations simply add a flavor element to the foundation while others can round out the Old World Comfort Mac and Cheese into a full meal. These first ten recipes do require baking or broiling which is in-line with the original recipe, so the only add prep time involves the additional ingredients in each recipe.

Options for these recipes, as well as the three other categories, include vegetarian options (though because of the cheese they are not completely vegan) as well as meat-filled options.

Mushroom Lover's Mac and Cheese

For those who love mushrooms, this recipe uses two of the more common and easily purchased types of mushrooms: Portobello and white button. Other mushroom varieties can be substituted as you desire. Mushroom purists may want to leave out the onion and garlic in the mushroom sauté.

More depth of flavor can be achieved by using a combination of truffle oil and olive oil during the sauté process or using 2 cups of grated truffle cheese in place of the water cheddar. It makes the dish quite a bit pricier but a richer delight. To make the dish a true adult version of a childhood favorite, serve with a nice French Burgundy, Rhone, or Pinot Noir.

Ingredients and Supplies

Pot of salted boiling water (Kosher salt works best)
Large skillet
Large saucepan
Large (2 quart) baking dish

8 ounces of pasta (Fusilli or Elbows)
½ pound sliced button (white) mushrooms
½ pound sliced and diced Portobello mushrooms
2 tablespoons of olive oil
½ yellow onion diced
1 tablespoon of diced garlic (or one clove)

4 tablespoons of unsalted butter
Additional teaspoon of salt

Non-stick spray or additional butter for baking dish

¼ cup all-purpose flour

2 cups of whole milk, warmed

Pinch of Nutmeg

1 bay leaf

2 cups of sharp white cheddar (or truffle cheese)

2 cups of Gruyere cheese (Keep ½ cup separate to top dish)

Directions

Preheat oven to 400 degrees.

Bring salted water to a boil.

Add pasta and cook until al dente, or slightly undercooked (it will finish while baking).

While pasta is cooking, heat the olive oil in a large skillet and add onions. Sauté for 2-3 minutes until the onions start to soften. Add mushrooms and continue to sauté. Add garlic 1 minute before removing from heat and onions have become translucent.

Drain pasta, leaving approximately 1 cup of water in with the pasta. This liquid will help the pasta to cook and thicken the final sauce.

In a large saucepan, melt 4 tablespoons of butter and whisk in flour over medium heat. After whisking flour for two minutes to create a paste, slowly whisk in the warmed milk. Add salt, nutmeg and bay leaf to the mix and whisk intermittently for 8 minutes. In a bowl, Combine 2 cups of white cheddar with the Gruyere and set aside.

Remove and discard the bay leaf. Add the cheeses to the saucepan. Combine the pasta, liquid and sauce by stirring. The mixture will be a loose consistency that will thicken up while baking.

Coat the baking dish with non-stick spray, butter, or vegetable oil. Pour the mixture into the dish and even the contents out across the dish. Pour the sautéed mushrooms over the pasta, and top with the remaining Gruyere cheddar cheese.

Bake for 15 minutes.

Onion Lovers' Mac and Cheese

This version of an onion lover' mac and cheese emphasizes the sweetness that comes out in caramelized onions while balancing the onion goodness in the freshness of scallions and the crunch of a fried onion topping. For adults, the Onion Lovers' Mac and Cheese builds on the white cheese base and goes well with white and light red wines. A heartier yellow cheese version of an onion Oktoberfest mac and cheese is part of the free bonuses available with this book at GinaLynnYummies.com and screams for a beer pairing.

Ingredients and Supplies
Pot of salted boiling water (Kosher salt works best)
Medium saucepan
Large saucepan
Large (2 quart) baking dish
Mixing bowl for cheeses

2 large yellow onions
8 tablespoons of unsalted butter

8 ounces of pasta (Fusilli or Elbows)
Additional teaspoon of salt
Non-stick spray or additional butter for baking dish
¼ cup all-purpose flour
2 cups of whole milk, warmed
Pinch of Nutmeg
1 bay leaf
2 ½ cups of sharp white cheddar (Keep ½ cup separate to top the dish)
1 ½ cups of Gruyere cheese

½ cup of canned fried onions
1 bunch of scallions

Directions

Slice 2 large yellow onions. Quarter the onion slices. Heat a medium saucepan and melt 4 tablespoons of unsalted butter over medium heat. Add onions to melted butter and lower heat. Cook onions until caramelized, stirring occasionally, approximately 15 minutes.

Preheat oven to 400 degrees.

Bring salted water to a boil.

Add pasta and cook until al dente, or slightly undercooked (it will finish while baking or broiling).

While pasta is cooking, melt remaining 4 tablespoons of butter and whisk in flour over medium heat. After whisking flour for two minutes to create a paste, slowly whisk in the warmed milk. Add salt, nutmeg and bay leaf to the mix and whisk intermittently for 8 minutes. In a bowl, Combine 2 cups of white cheddar with the Gruyere and set aside.

Drain pasta, leaving approximately 1 cup of water in with the pasta. This liquid will help the pasta to cook and thicken the final sauce. Stir in half of the chopped scallions.

Return to the saucepan, remove and discard the bay leaf. Add the blended cheeses to the saucepan. Combine the pasta, liquid and sauce by stirring. The mixture will be a looser, liquid consistency which will thicken up while baking.

Coat the baking dish with non-stick spray, butter, or vegetable oil. Add the pasta and cheese sauce to the dish. Evenly distribute the onion mixture into the dish using a fork, tongs or slotted spoon to avoid the extra level of greasiness with the butter added to the sauce. Top with the remaining cheddar cheese and a sprinkle of the fried onions.

Bake for 15 minutes.

Plate and top with remaining chopped scallions.

Spinach Artichoke Mac and Cheese

If you like spinach artichoke dip, you'll love this recipe that takes your favorite appetizer and makes it into a satisfying side dish or tasty meatless main course.

Ingredients and Supplies
Pot of salted boiling water (Kosher salt works best)
Large saucepan
Large (2 quart) baking dish
Mixing bowl for cheeses
Small bowl to mix topping

8 ounces of pasta (Fusilli or Elbows)
4 tablespoons of unsalted butter
Additional teaspoon of salt
Non-stick spray or additional butter for baking dish
¼ cup all-purpose flour
2 cups of whole milk, warmed
Pinch of Nutmeg
1 bay leaf
2 ½ cups of sharp white cheddar (Keep ½ cup separate to top the dish)
1 ½ cups of Gruyere cheese

6 oz. jar of marinated artichoke hearts
1 cup chopped baby spinach

For topping:
2 tablespoons Panko
2 tablespoons of grated parmesan

1 tablespoon of dried parsley or 2 tablespoons of
fresh chopped parsley

Directions
Preheat oven to 400 degrees.
Bring salted water to a boil.
Add pasta and cook until al dente, or slightly
undercooked (it will finish while baking or
broiling).

While pasta is cooking, melt 4 tablespoons of
butter and whisk in flour over medium heat. After
whisking flour for two minutes to create a paste, slowly
whisk in the warmed milk. Add salt, nutmeg and bay
leaf to the mix and whisk intermittently for 8 minutes.
In a bowl, Combine 2 cups of white cheddar with the
Gruyere and set aside.

Drain pasta, leaving approximately 1 cup of
water in with the pasta. This liquid will help the pasta to
cook and thicken the final sauce.

Return to the saucepan, remove and discard the
bay leaf. Add the blended cheeses to the saucepan.
Combine the pasta, all of the reserved pasta liquid and
sauce by stirring. The mixture will be a loose
consistency that will thicken up while baking.

Dice the artichoke hearts and add them to the
pasta mix along with the chopped baby spinach. Stir to
make sure the vegetables are distributed throughout the
pasta.

Coat the baking dish with non-stick spray,
butter, or vegetable oil. Pour the mixture into the dish

and even the contents out across the dish. Combine, Panko, Parmesan, and parsley in a small bowl. Sprinkle the remaining cheddar cheese on the pasta with the topping as the final layer.

Bake for 15 minutes.

Italian Basics Mac and Cheese

This is an Italian twist on the basic Old World, White Cheese recipe. It is an appealing stand alone or can be the foundation for additional ingredients such as diced sun dried tomatoes and olives.

Ingredients and Supplies
Pot of salted boiling water (Kosher salt works best)
Large saucepan
Large (2 quart) baking dish
Mixing bowl for cheeses

8 ounces of pasta (Fusilli or Elbows)
4 tablespoons of unsalted butter
Additional teaspoon of salt
Non-stick spray or additional butter for baking dish
¼ cup all-purpose flour
2 cups of whole milk, warmed
Pinch of Nutmeg
1 bay leaf
2 ½ cups of Fontina cheese (Keep ½ cup separate to top the dish)
1 ½ cups of Gruyere cheese
1 tablespoon Italian seasoning

Topping:
¼ cup of Panko
¼ cup grated Parmesan cheese

Directions
Preheat oven to 400 degrees.
Bring salted water to a boil.

Add pasta and cook until al dente, or slightly undercooked (it will finish while baking or broiling).

While pasta is cooking, melt 4 tablespoons of butter and whisk in flour over medium heat. After whisking flour for two minutes to create a paste, slowly whisk in the warmed milk. Add salt, nutmeg and bay leaf to the mix and whisk intermittently for 8 minutes. In a bowl, Combine 2 cups of Fontina with the Gruyere and set aside.

Drain pasta, leaving approximately 1 cup of water in with the pasta. This liquid will help the pasta to cook and thicken the final sauce.

Return to the saucepan, remove and discard the bay leaf. Add the blended cheeses to the saucepan. Combine the pasta, liquid, sauce, and Italian seasoning by stirring. The mixture will be a loose consistency that will thicken up while baking.

Coat the baking dish with non-stick spray, butter, or vegetable oil. Pour the mixture into the dish and even the contents out across the dish. Mix Panko and Parmesan. Top with the remaining Fontina cheese with a layer of the cheddar cheese as finishing touch.

Bake for 15 minutes.

Plate and season to taste with salt and pepper.

Fruity French Mac and Cheese

This is a slightly unexpected and naturally sweeter version of mac and cheese. The surprising taste profile pairs well with white wines such as Rieslings and Gewürztraminers. It can serve as an interesting appetizer as well as a side dish for salty and spicier dishes, such as ham or meat and vegetable dishes that have the heat of red pepper flakes or Siracha.

Ingredients and Supplies
Pot of salted boiling water (Kosher salt works best)
Large saucepan
Large (2 quart) baking dish
Mixing bowl for cheeses

8 ounces of pasta (Fusilli or Elbows)
4 tablespoons of unsalted butter
Additional teaspoon of salt
Non-stick spray or additional butter for baking dish
¼ cup all-purpose flour
2 cups of whole milk, warmed
Pinch of Nutmeg
1 bay leaf
8 oz. brie (Rind Removed)
2 cups of Gruyere cheese (1/2 cup reserved for topping)

2 cups chopped walnuts
1 cup diced dates (or dried figs)

Directions
Preheat oven to 400 degrees.
Bring salted water to a boil.
Add pasta and cook until al dente, or slightly undercooked (it will finish while baking or broiling).

While pasta is cooking, melt 4 tablespoons of butter and whisk in flour over medium heat. After whisking flour for two minutes to create a paste, slowly whisk in the warmed milk. Add salt, nutmeg and bay leaf to the mix and whisk intermittently for 8 minutes.

Drain pasta, leaving approximately 1 cup of water in with the pasta. This liquid will help the pasta to cook and thicken the final sauce.

Return to the saucepan, remove and discard the bay leaf. Add the blended cheeses to the saucepan. Combine the pasta, cheeses, and pasta liquid by stirring. The mixture will be a loose consistency that will thicken up while baking.

Chop walnuts and dates or figs. Add them to the pasta and stir to be sure everything is integrated.

Coat the baking dish with non-stick spray, butter, or vegetable oil. Pour the mixture into the dish and even the contents out across the dish. Top with the remaining Gruyere cheese.

Bake for 15 minutes.

Lobster Mac and Cheese

This is one of the ultimate, decadent, adult versions of a childhood favorite. To make it a truly adult dish, pair it with an ice cold bottle of bubbly and see how the food and wine make a match straight from heaven.

Ingredients and Supplies
Pot of salted boiling water (Kosher salt works best)
Large saucepan
Large (2 quart) baking dish
Small mixing bowl for topping

8 ounces of pasta (Fusilli or Elbows)
4 tablespoons of unsalted butter
1 tablespoon of melted unsalted butter
Additional teaspoon of salt
Non-stick spray or additional butter for baking dish
¼ cup all-purpose flour
2 cups of whole milk, warmed
Pinch of Nutmeg
1 bay leaf
2 ½ cups of sharp white cheddar (Keep ½ cup separate to top the dish)
1 ½ cups of Gruyere cheese

12 oz. lobster meat, cooked and chunked
½ cup Panko
¼ cup chopped chives

Directions
Preheat oven to broil.

Bring salted water to a boil.
Add pasta and cook until al dente.

While pasta is cooking, melt 4 tablespoons of butter and whisk in flour over medium heat. After whisking flour for two minutes to create a paste, slowly whisk in the warmed milk. Add salt, nutmeg and bay leaf to the mix and whisk intermittently for 8 minutes. In a bowl, Combine 2 cups of white cheddar with the Gruyere and set aside.

Drain pasta, leaving approximately 1 cup of water in with the pasta. This liquid will help the pasta to cook and thicken the final sauce.

Return to the saucepan, remove and discard the bay leaf. Add the blended cheeses to the saucepan. Combine the pasta, liquid and sauce by stirring. The mixture should be loose without being overly liquid.

Mix lobster into the pasta. Mix the Panko and chives together in a small bowl for topping.

Coat the baking dish with non-stick spray, butter, or vegetable oil. Pour the mixture into the dish and even the contents out across the dish. Top with the remaining cheese and then a layer of the Panko mix. Drizzle melted butter over the top.

Broil until golden brown on top.

Garlic Salmon Mac and Cheese

This hearty and tasty salmon based mac and cheese provides a meatier seafood mac and cheese experience compared to the lobster version. Because salmon is more robust in flavor, this dish works well with a Pinot Noir instead of a bubbly. For an added dimension of flavor, use roasted garlic. (Instructions for roasting garlic follow the recipe.) The dish can be prepared quickly by using a canned salmon. Otherwise, the salmon will need to be cooked before preparing the dish.

Ingredients and Supplies
Pot of salted boiling water (Kosher salt works best)
Large saucepan
Large (2 quart) baking dish
Small mixing bowl for topping

8 ounces of pasta (Fusilli or Elbows)
4 tablespoons of unsalted butter
1 tablespoon of melted unsalted butter
Additional teaspoon of salt
Non-stick spray or additional butter for baking dish
¼ cup all-purpose flour
2 cups of whole milk, warmed
Pinch of Nutmeg
1 bay leaf
2 ½ cups of sharp white cheddar (Keep ½ cup separate to top the dish)
1 ½ cups of Gruyere cheese

10 oz. of cooked salmon

½ chopped red onion
2 cloves of chopped garlic (approximately 3
cloves of roasted garlic)
½ cup Panko
¼ cup chopped chives

Directions
Preheat oven to broil.
Bring salted water to a boil.
Add pasta and cook until al dente.

While pasta is cooking, melt 4 tablespoons of butter and whisk in flour over medium heat. After whisking flour for two minutes to create a paste, slowly whisk in the warmed milk. Add salt, nutmeg and bay leaf to the mix and whisk intermittently for 8 minutes. In a bowl, Combine 2 cups of white cheddar with the Gruyere and set aside.

Drain pasta, leaving approximately 1 cup of water in with the pasta. This liquid will help the pasta to cook and thicken the final sauce.

Return to the saucepan, remove and discard the bay leaf. Add the blended cheeses to the saucepan. Combine the pasta, liquid and sauce by stirring. The mixture should be loose without being overly liquid.

Mix salmon, garlic, and onion into the pasta. Mix the Panko and chives together in a small bowl for topping.

Coat the baking dish with non-stick spray, butter, or vegetable oil. Pour the mixture into the dish and even the contents out across the dish. Top with the remaining cheese and then a layer of the Panko mix. Drizzle melted butter over the top.

Broil until golden brown on top.

Roasted Garlic

Making roasted garlic is easy and it is a great addition to a wide range of dishes.

Instructions

You will need 1 or more bulbs of garlic, olive oil, and salt along with a small baking dish.

Heat you oven to 425 degrees.

Cut the top off the garlic bulb, attempting to slice the top off of as many cloves as possible.

Place garlic in the dish. Drizzle with olive oil, and sprinkle with salt.

Roast until the top and outside of the bulb in a golden brown, and the bulb is soft to the touch.

The roasted garlic should have a mushy paste consistency.

Supreme Pizza Mac and Cheese

This dish allows you to combine the pleasures of pizza with the comfort of mac and cheese. This recipe uses pepperoni, but you can substitute or add some cooked sausage crumbs to make it a true supreme pizza experience.

Ingredients and Supplies
Pot of salted boiling water (Kosher salt works best)
Large saucepan
Large (2 quart) baking dish
Small mixing bowl for topping

8 ounces of pasta (Fusilli or Elbows)
4 tablespoons of unsalted butter
1 tablespoon of melted unsalted butter
Additional teaspoon of salt
Non-stick spray or additional butter for baking dish
¼ cup all-purpose flour
2 cups of whole milk, warmed
Pinch of Nutmeg
1 bay leaf
2 cups of sharp white cheddar (Keep ½ cup separate to top the dish)
1 ½ cups of Gruyere cheese
½ cup of Mozzarella cheese (smoked if preferred)

10 oz. of chopped pepperoni (and or crumbled cooked Italian sausage)
½ medium yellow onion, chopped
½ medium green bell pepper, chopped

½ cup roasted red pepper, sliced
¼ cup black olives, sliced and drained
1 clove garlic, diced
1 tablespoon of dried oregano or Italian seasonings

Directions
Preheat oven to broil.
Bring salted water to a boil.
Add pasta and cook until al dente.

While pasta is cooking, melt 4 tablespoons of butter and whisk in flour over medium heat. After whisking flour for two minutes to create a paste, slowly whisk in the warmed milk. Add salt, nutmeg and bay leaf to the mix and whisk intermittently for 8 minutes. In a bowl, Combine 1 1/2 cups of white cheddar with the Gruyere and Mozzarella and set aside.

Drain pasta, leaving approximately 1 cup of water in with the pasta. This liquid will help the pasta to cook and thicken the final sauce.

Return to the saucepan, remove and discard the bay leaf. Add the blended cheeses to the saucepan. Combine the pasta, liquid and sauce by stirring. The mixture should be loose without being overly liquid.

Mix pepperoni, onions, peppers, olives, garlic and seasonings into the pasta.

Coat the baking dish with butter or oil. Pour the mixture into the dish and even the contents out across the dish. Top with the remaining cheddar cheese.

Broil until golden brown on top.

Southwest Shredded Beef Mac and Cheese

This dish is a great way to take care of leftover roasts. If you don't have roast beef around to shred, you can substitute diced sandwich meats or substitute chicken for the beef as well. For added crunch to the dish, a layer of corn chips is added over the top.

Ingredients and Supplies
Pot of salted boiling water (Kosher salt works best)
Large saucepan
Large (2 quart) baking dish
Mixing bowl for cheeses

8 ounces of pasta (Fusilli or Elbows)
4 tablespoons of unsalted butter
Additional teaspoon of salt
Non-stick spray or additional butter for baking dish
¼ cup all-purpose flour
2 cups of whole milk, warmed
Pinch of Nutmeg
1 bay leaf
2 ½ cups white cheddar cheese (1/2 cup reserved for topping)
1 ½ cups of pepper jack cheese

3 cups of shredded beef
¼ cup of diced green chilies
½ medium white onion, diced
1 tablespoon of taco seasoning
½ corn chips, crushed

Directions

Preheat oven to 400 degrees.

Bring salted water to a boil.

Add pasta and cook until al dente, or slightly undercooked (it will finish while baking or broiling).

While pasta is cooking, melt 4 tablespoons of butter and whisk in flour over medium heat. After whisking flour for two minutes to create a paste, slowly whisk in the warmed milk. Add salt, nutmeg and bay leaf to the mix and whisk intermittently for 8 minutes.

Drain pasta, leaving approximately 1 cup of water in with the pasta. This liquid will help the pasta to cook and thicken the final sauce.

Return to the saucepan, remove and discard the bay leaf. Add the blended cheeses to the saucepan. Combine the pasta, cheeses, and pasta liquid by stirring. The mixture will be a loose, slightly liquid consistency that will thicken up while baking.

Mix beef, green chilies, and onions into the pasta.

Coat the baking dish with non-stick spray, butter, or vegetable oil. Pour the mixture into the dish and even the contents out across the dish. Top with the remaining cheddar cheese and sprinkle taco seasoning over the top.

Bake for 15 minutes.

Reuben Mac and Cheese

This dish is a unique combination of a deli favorite with beloved pasta dish. Though Reuben sandwiches traditionally have Swiss cheese, this recipe substitutes Gruyere for Swiss to maintain the melted goodness.

Ingredients and Supplies
Pot of salted boiling water (Kosher salt works best)
Large saucepan
Large (2 quart) baking dish
Mixing bowl for cheeses

8 ounces of pasta (Fusilli or Elbows)
4 tablespoons of unsalted butter
Additional teaspoon of salt
Non-stick spray or additional butter for baking dish
¼ cup all-purpose flour
2 cups of whole milk, warmed
Pinch of Nutmeg
1 bay leaf
2 ½ cups of white cheddar cheese (Keep ½ cup separate to top the dish)
1 ½ cups of Gruyere cheese

3 cups of cooked corned beef, diced into bite sized pieces
1 cup of drained, packed, and diced sauerkraut
¼ cup of Thousand Island dressing

Directions
Preheat oven to 400 degrees.

Bring salted water to a boil.

Add pasta and cook until al dente, or slightly undercooked (it will finish while baking or broiling).

While pasta is cooking, melt 4 tablespoons of butter and whisk in flour over medium heat. After whisking flour for two minutes to create a paste, slowly whisk in the warmed milk. Add salt, nutmeg and bay leaf to the mix and whisk intermittently for 8 minutes. In a bowl, Combine 2 cups of Fontina with the Gruyere and set aside.

Drain pasta, reserving approximately 1/2 cup of pasta. This liquid will help the pasta to cook and thicken the final sauce.

Return to the saucepan, remove and discard the bay leaf. Stir the blended cheeses into the saucepan. Add pasta and dressing while continuing to stir. Add reserved pasta liquid slowly as you stir.

Combine corned beef and sauerkraut with the pasta until mixed through.

Coat the baking dish with non-stick spray, butter, or vegetable oil. Pour the mixture into the dish and even the contents out across the dish. Top with the remaining cheese as the finishing touch.

Bake for 15 minutes.

8 Options to Pump up the Parma-Alfredo Mac and Cheese

Don't want fire up the oven or heat up the broiler? No problem. We have stove top friendly recipes that use a white cheese, Alfredo base that will have your taste delighting to vegetarian friendly dishes as well as chicken dishes to satisfy your inner carnivore.

All recipes in this section use the Parma-Alfredo Mac and Cheese base with minor variations as necessary. With the exception of dishes that include cooked meats, these one pot wonders can be made in 15-20 minutes tops. To keep cooking times short, even with meat dishes, meat from a store bought and roasted chicken can be used.

Pesto Mac and Cheese

This pesto piece works well on and it is versatile enough to serve as an additional base for easy jazz ups. Toasted pine nuts can be added while keeping the dish vegetarian friendly. For those who want to add animal protein, 2 cups of cooked shrimp or 2 cups of chopped, cooked chicken can round out the dish into a meal of its own.

Ingredients and Supplies

Pot of salted boiling water (Kosher salt works best)
Large skillet

8 ounces of pasta (Penne or other small pasta)
1 garlic clove
1 tablespoon unsalted butter
2 cups heavy cream
1/2 cup shredded Parmigiano-Reggiano (Parmesan) cheese for sauce
2 tablespoons of Pesto (3 tablespoons if adding meat)
½ cup of fresh basil, chopped

1/4 cup of Parmigiano-Reggiano (Parmesan) cheese for topping
1 teaspoon of salt and pepper, plus more to taste

Directions

Bring salted water to a boil.
Add pasta and cook until al dente.
Reserve 1 cup of pasta liquid for sauce.
Drain pasta.

Smash the garlic clove on a cutting board with the side of a large Chef's knife. Rub the skillet with the garlic and toss the clove. Heat the skillet over medium heat and melt the butter. Add the heavy cream and salt and pepper (approximately one teaspoon). Reduce to a low heat and let simmer about 5 minutes until the mixture reduces by about 30%. Stir in ½ cup of Parmigiano-Reggiano followed by the pasta. Add some of the reserved pasta liquid to thicken sauce. Stir until sauce is creamy and cheese is melted. When the mixture is creamy, incorporate pesto, basil and meat (if you are adding it).

Plate, season with salt and pepper to taste, and top with additional cheese.

Garlic-Herb Goodness Mac and Cheese

Much like the Pesto Mac and Cheese, this Garlic-Herb Goodness can be served on its own or serve as the base for additional items like chicken, shrimp and salmon.

Ingredients and Supplies

Pot of salted boiling water (Kosher salt works best)
Large skillet
Small skillet

8 ounces of pasta (Penne or other small pasta)
1 garlic clove
1 tablespoon unsalted butter
2 cups heavy cream
1/2 cup shredded Parmigiano-Reggiano (Parmesan) cheese for sauce
1/4 cup of Parmigiano-Reggiano (Parmesan) cheese for topping
1 teaspoon of salt and pepper, plus more to taste

1 clove of garlic, minced
1 tablespoon unsalted butter
1 teaspoon of chopped basil
1 teaspoon of chopped chives
1 teaspoon of parsley
1 teaspoon of thyme

Directions

Bring salted water to a boil.
Add pasta and cook until al dente.

While pasta is cooking, melt one table spoon of butter. Sauté the garlic and herbs (basil, chives, parley, and thyme) for one minute and then turn off the heat. The mixture will be added to the pasta at the end.

Reserve 1 cup of pasta liquid for sauce.
Drain pasta.

Smash the garlic clove on a cutting board with the side of a large Chef's knife. Rub the skillet with the garlic and toss the clove. Heat the skillet over medium heat and melt the butter. Add the heavy cream and salt and pepper (approximately one teaspoon). Reduce to a low heat and let simmer about 5 minutes until the mixture reduces by about 30%. Stir in ½ cup of Parmigiano-Reggiano followed by the pasta. Add some of the reserved pasta liquid to thicken sauce and stir until sauce is creamy and cheese is melted. Transfer the garlic and herb mixture from the small skillet and mix together.

Plate, season with salt and pepper to taste, and top with additional cheese.

Greek Mac and Cheese

This Greek inspired dish combines a bit of the Italian tradition with that of Greece. Using Kalamata olives rather than standard black olives can give this dish a punched up flavor as well more authenticity. If you do substitute Calamatas, remember they have pits in them or take the time to remove the pits and dice them beforehand or use a tapenade. To avoid being overwhelmed by the Calamites, reduce the portion to 6 large olives or a generous tablespoon of the tapenade.

Ingredients and Supplies

Pot of salted boiling water (Kosher salt works best)

Large skillet

8 ounces of pasta (Penne or other small pasta)

1 garlic clove

1 tablespoon unsalted butter

2 cups heavy cream

1/2 cup shredded Parmigiano-Reggiano (Parmesan) cheese for sauce

1/4 cup of Parmigiano-Reggiano (Parmesan) cheese for topping

1 teaspoon of salt and pepper, plus more to taste

4 ounces Feta cheese, cubes or crumbs

¼ cup sun-dried tomatoes, chopped

¼ cup of black olives, sliced

1 tablespoon oregano

Directions

Bring salted water to a boil.

Add pasta and cook until al dente.
Reserve 1 cup of pasta liquid for sauce.
Drain pasta.

Smash the garlic clove on a cutting board with the side of a large Chef's knife. Rub the skillet with the garlic and toss the clove. Heat the skillet over medium heat and melt the butter. Add the heavy cream and salt and pepper (approximately one teaspoon). Reduce to a low heat and let simmer about 5 minutes until the mixture reduces by about 30%. Stir in ½ cup of Parmigiano-Reggiano followed by the pasta. Add some of the reserved pasta liquid to thicken sauce and stir until sauce is creamy and cheese is melted.

Add Feta, olives, tomatoes, and oregano, and stir until mixed through.

Plate, season with salt and pepper to taste, and top with additional cheese.

Velvety Veggie Mac and Cheese

This is a quick way to add some veggies into your meal in a way that will make both children and adult happy. The easiest option is to use frozen mixed vegetables that have been heated for service. While that is the simplest way to "veggie up" this mac and cheese, you can use canned or any other cooked vegetables that you desire.

Ingredients and Supplies
Pot of salted boiling water (Kosher salt works best)
Large skillet

8 ounces of pasta (Penne or other small pasta)
1 garlic clove
1 tablespoon unsalted butter
2 cups heavy cream
1/2 cup shredded Parmigiano-Reggiano (Parmesan) cheese for sauce
1/4 cup of Parmigiano-Reggiano (Parmesan) cheese for topping
1 teaspoon of salt and pepper, plus more to taste

2 cups frozen mixed vegetables, warmed and ready to eat
2 tablespoons Mascarpone cheese
2 tablespoons parsley

Directions
Bring salted water to a boil.
Add pasta and cook until al dente.
Reserve 1 cup of pasta liquid for sauce.
Drain pasta.

Smash the garlic clove on a cutting board with the side of a large Chef's knife. Rub the skillet with the garlic and toss the clove. Heat the skillet over medium heat and melt the butter. Add the heavy cream and salt and pepper (approximately one teaspoon). Reduce to a low heat and let simmer about 5 minutes until the mixture reduces by about 30%. Stir in ½ cup of Parmigiano-Reggiano followed by the pasta. Add some of the reserved pasta liquid to thicken sauce and stir until sauce is creamy and cheese is melted.

Add warmed vegetables and Mascarpone and stir thoroughly.

Plate and season with salt and pepper to taste. Top with additional cheese and parsley.

Quad-Cheese Mac and Cheese

When it's time to seriously get your cheese on, this four cheese version hits the spot. The Italian cheeses of Parmigiano-Reggiano, Mozzarella, Asiago, and Teleggio combine to create a truly cheesy punch.

Ingredients and Supplies
Pot of salted boiling water (Kosher salt works best)
Large skillet
Small skillet for quick sauté

8 ounces of pasta (Penne or other small pasta)
1 garlic clove
1 tablespoon unsalted butter
2 cups heavy cream
1/2 cup shredded Parmigiano-Reggiano (Parmesan) cheese for sauce
1/4 cup of Parmigiano-Reggiano (Parmesan) cheese for topping
1 teaspoon of salt and pepper, plus more to taste

1 tablespoon of unsalted butter
1 shallot, minced
2 tablespoons parsley, chopped or dried
¼ cup shredded Mozzarella
¼ cup shredded Asiago
¼ cup cubed Teleggio

Directions
Bring salted water to a boil.
Add pasta and cook until al dente.

Sauté the minced shallot in 1 tablespoon of butter and set aside for later

Reserve 1 cup of pasta liquid for sauce.
Drain pasta.

Smash the garlic clove on a cutting board with the side of a large Chef's knife. Rub the skillet with the garlic and toss the clove. Heat the skillet over medium heat and melt the butter. Add the heavy cream and salt and pepper (approximately one teaspoon). Reduce to a low heat and let simmer about 5 minutes until the mixture reduces by about 30%. Stir in ½ cup of Parmigiano-Reggiano followed by the pasta. Add some of the reserved pasta liquid to thicken sauce and stir until sauce is creamy and cheese is melted.

Stir in Teleggio cubes. When the cubes have softened and started to melt, add Asiago, followed by Mozzarella. Continue stirring until additional cheeses are melted into the sauce.

Plate, season with salt and pepper to taste, and top with additional cheese.

Chicken Florentine Mac and Cheese

Maximize the Italian influences in mac and cheese with this ode to the Florentine tradition which combines all the food groups into a single dish. With the use of a pre-roasted chicken, the dish can come together in a matter of minutes.

Ingredients and Supplies
Pot of salted boiling water (Kosher salt works best)
Large skillet

8 ounces of pasta (Penne or other small pasta)
1 garlic clove
1 tablespoon unsalted butter
2 cups heavy cream
1/2 cup shredded Parmigiano-Reggiano (Parmesan) cheese for sauce
1/4 cup of Parmigiano-Reggiano (Parmesan) cheese for topping
1 teaspoon of salt and pepper, plus more to taste

2 cups cooked chicken, shredded or chopped
¼ cup sun-dried tomatoes, chopped
2 cups baby spinach

Directions
Bring salted water to a boil.
Add pasta and cook until al dente.
Reserve 1 cup of pasta liquid for sauce.
Drain pasta.

Smash the garlic clove on a cutting board with the side of a large Chef's knife. Rub the skillet with the garlic and toss the clove. Heat the skillet over medium heat and melt the butter. Add the heavy cream and salt and pepper (approximately one teaspoon). Reduce to a low heat and let simmer about 5 minutes until the mixture reduces by about 30%. Stir in ½ cup of Parmigiano-Reggiano followed by the pasta. Add some of the reserved pasta liquid to thicken sauce and stir until sauce is creamy and cheese is melted.

Add in spinach and stir until leaves are coated and warmed. The spinach will cook down and shrink as it heats. Stir in chicken and tomatoes when spinach is incorporated.

Plate, season with salt and pepper to taste, and top with additional cheese.

Pan-Pea Mac and Cheese

This dish is a pleasing yet sophisticated mix of cheese, peas, and pancetta which is a culinary comfort that people of all ages can appreciate and enjoy.

Ingredients and Supplies
Pot of salted boiling water (Kosher salt works best)
Large skillet

8 ounces of pasta (Penne or other small pasta)
1 garlic clove
1 tablespoon unsalted butter
2 cups heavy cream
1/2 cup shredded Parmigiano-Reggiano (Parmesan) cheese for sauce
1/4 cup of Parmigiano-Reggiano (Parmesan) cheese for topping
1 teaspoon of salt and pepper, plus more to taste

1 15 oz. can of sweet peas, drained
2 ounces of chopped pancetta
1 tablespoon of parsley

Directions
Bring salted water to a boil.
Add pasta and cook until al dente.

Reserve 1 cup of pasta liquid for sauce.
Drain pasta.

Smash the garlic clove on a cutting board with the side of a large Chef's knife. Rub the skillet with the garlic and toss the clove. Heat the skillet over medium heat and melt the butter. Cook pancetta.

Add the heavy cream and salt and pepper (approximately one teaspoon). Reduce to a low heat and let simmer about 5 minutes until the mixture reduces by about 30%. Stir in ½ cup of Parmigiano-Reggiano followed by the pasta. Add some of the reserved pasta liquid to thicken sauce and stir until sauce is creamy and cheese is melted.

Stir in peas.

Plate, season with salt and pepper to taste, and top with additional cheese.

Harvest Chicken Mac and Cheese

This unexpected taste sensation celebrates the fall season but is a welcome quick fix year around. The combination of apple, walnuts, and chicken sausage gives a different dimension to the Parma-Alfredo mac and cheese base.

Ingredients and Supplies
Pot of salted boiling water (Kosher salt works best)
Large skillet

8 ounces of pasta (Penne or other small pasta)
1 garlic clove
1 tablespoon unsalted butter
2 cups heavy cream
1/2 cup shredded Parmigiano-Reggiano (Parmesan) cheese for sauce
1/4 cup of Parmigiano-Reggiano (Parmesan) cheese for topping
1 teaspoon of salt and pepper, plus more to taste

2 cups of chicken sausage, sliced and cooked
1 cup green apple, diced
¼ walnuts, chopped

Directions
Bring salted water to a boil.
Add pasta and cook until al dente.
Reserve 1 cup of pasta liquid for sauce.
Drain pasta.

Smash the garlic clove on a cutting board with the side of a large Chef's knife. Rub the skillet with the garlic and toss the clove. Heat the skillet over medium heat and melt the butter. Add the heavy cream and salt and pepper (approximately one teaspoon). Reduce to a low heat and let simmer about 5 minutes until the mixture reduces by about 30%. Stir in ½ cup of Parmigiano-Reggiano followed by the pasta. Add some of the reserved pasta liquid to thicken sauce and stir until sauce is creamy and cheese is melted.

Stir in cooked chicken sausage, apple, and walnuts. Continue stirring until warmed through.

Plate, season with salt and pepper to taste, and top with additional cheese.

8 Eat'em Up, No-Bake Yellow Mac and Cheese Options

For those who grew up with the ubiquitous boxed mac and cheese, the New World Comfort No-Bake Mac and Cheese is the American favorite. Forget the pre-fab meal in a box, this is homemade comfort food. Though the mac and cheese base for these options is no-bake, three of the options included in the coming pages do require some bake time. Even with the extra step, you'll love the tasty, cheesy goodness that can be served as either a side or main dish.

.

Cheesy Trees Mac and Cheese

Moms know that one way to get kids to eat broccoli to melt some cheese over it. Take the trick one step further by making a mac and cheese with broccoli. Better yet, make it fit the tastes of both young and old to a tee with Havarti. To increase the appeal, add ½ cup (about 4 slices) of crumbled bacon to send the dish over the top for everyone.

Ingredients and Supplies
Pot of salted boiling water (Kosher salt works
    best)
Medium saucepan

8 ounces of pasta (Elbows or Fusilli)
1 tablespoon of unsalted butter
1 tablespoon all-purpose flour
1 teaspoon mustard powder
Cayenne pepper to taste or hot sauce such as
    Tapatio (optional)
12 oz. evaporated milk
1 ½ cups Havarti
¼ cubed processed cheese
2 cups broccoli florets
Salt and pepper to taste

Directions
Bring salted water to a boil.
Add pasta and cook until al dente.
Reserve 1 cup of pasta liquid for sauce.
Drain pasta.

In the saucepan, melt butter. Over medium heat, whisk in flour, mustard powder, and cayenne or hot sauce. Whisk for 1 minute before slowly incorporating evaporated milk and whisk to thoroughly mix. Lower heat to a simmer and whisk intermittently for about 5 minutes as sauce begins to thicken. Stir in both cheeses and broccoli. Add enough reserved pasta liquid to further thicken the sauce for at least 3 minutes.

Plate the mac and cheese. Season with salt and pepper to taste.

Peas and Ham Mac and Cheese

This quick and easy, one-pot, people-pleaser works well as a main dish as well as a side for all kinds of occasions.

Ingredients and Supplies
Pot of salted boiling water (Kosher salt works best)
Medium saucepan

8 ounces of pasta (Elbows or Fusilli)
1 tablespoon of unsalted butter
1 tablespoon all-purpose flour
1 teaspoon mustard powder
Cayenne pepper to taste or hot sauce such as Tapatio (optional)
12 oz. evaporated milk
1 ½ cups grated yellow cheddar cheese (mild is most universal, but medium, sharp or smoked can add a depth of flavor)
¼ cubed processed cheese
1 15 oz. can of sweet peas, drained
1 ½ cups of chopped ham
Salt and pepper to taste

Directions
Bring salted water to a boil.
Add pasta and cook until al dente.
Reserve 1 cup of pasta liquid for sauce.
Drain pasta.

In the saucepan, melt butter. Over medium heat, whisk in flour, mustard powder, and cayenne or hot sauce. Whisk for 1 minute before slowly incorporating evaporated milk and whisk to thoroughly mix. Lower heat to a simmer and whisk intermittently for about 5 minutes as sauce begins to thicken. Stir in both cheeses. Add enough reserved pasta liquid to further thicken the sauce.

Stir in ham and peas until warmed through.

Plate the mac and cheese. Season with salt and pepper to taste.

Taco Tuesday Mac and Cheese

Facing another Taco Tuesday? Take a typical school night meal in a different direction with the Taco Tuesday Mac and Cheese. Don't worry. Your secret's safe if you decide to try a taco treat another day of the week.

Ingredients and Supplies
Pot of salted boiling water (Kosher salt works best)
Medium saucepan and skillet

8 ounces of pasta (Elbows or Fusilli)
1 tablespoon of unsalted butter
1 tablespoon all-purpose flour
1 teaspoon mustard powder
Cayenne pepper to taste or hot sauce such as Tapatio (optional)
12 oz. evaporated milk
1 ½ cups grated yellow cheddar cheese
¼ cubed processed cheese
½ lb. of ground beef or turkey
2 tablespoons Taco Seasoning
¼ prepared red salsa
¼ cup white onion, chopped
¼ cup of cilantro, chopped

Directions

Cook the ground meat with Taco Seasoning on high in a medium skillet.
Drain.

Bring salted water to a boil.
Add pasta and cook until al dente.
Reserve 1 cup of pasta liquid for sauce.
Drain pasta.

In the saucepan, melt butter. Over medium heat, whisk in flour, mustard powder, and cayenne or hot sauce. Whisk for 1 minute before slowly incorporating evaporated milk and whisk to thoroughly mix. Lower heat to a simmer and whisk intermittently for about 5 minutes as sauce begins to thicken. Stir in both cheeses. Add enough reserved pasta liquid to further thicken the sauce.

Stir in cooked meat and salsa. Continue to mix until warmed through.

Plate the mac and cheese. Top with onions and cilantro.

BBQ Pulled Pork Mac and Cheese

Southeast meets southwest in this fusion of all kinds of southern comfort food. Green chilies balance out the sweetness of the barbequed pork in this cheesy goodness that makes people of all ages smile. This is a simple way to use up pulled pork leftovers. If you don't have leftovers, you can often find barbequed pulled pork or beef ready made in grocery stores to make things easier.

Ingredients and Supplies
Pot of salted boiling water (Kosher salt works best)
Medium saucepan

8 ounces of pasta (Elbows or Fusilli)
1 tablespoon of unsalted butter
1 tablespoon all-purpose flour
1 teaspoon mustard powder
Cayenne pepper to taste or hot sauce such as Tapatio (optional)
12 oz. evaporated milk
1 ½ cups grated yellow cheddar cheese (mild is most universal, but medium, sharp or smoked can add a depth of flavor)
¼ cubed processed cheese
1 cup barbequed pulled pork (or beef), prepared
2 tablespoons canned green chilies
Salt and pepper to taste

Directions
Bring salted water to a boil.
Add pasta and cook until al dente.
Reserve 1 cup of pasta liquid for sauce.

Drain pasta.

In the saucepan, melt butter. Over medium heat, whisk in flour, mustard powder, and cayenne or hot sauce. Whisk for 1 minute before slowly incorporating evaporated milk and whisk to thoroughly mix. Lower heat to a simmer and whisk intermittently for about 5 minutes as sauce begins to thicken. Stir in both cheeses. Add enough reserved pasta liquid to further thicken the sauce.

Add meat and green chilies and stir until warmed through.

Plate the mac and cheese. Season with salt and pepper to taste.

Cajun Mac and Cheese

Bring a little bit of the bayou into your dining room with this spicy, flavorful mac and cheese dish that is good enough to have you partying in the streets like it's Fat Tuesday, any day of the year.

Ingredients and Supplies
Pot of salted boiling water (Kosher salt works best)
Medium saucepan
Medium skillet

8 ounces of pasta (Elbows or Fusilli)
1 tablespoon of unsalted butter
1 tablespoon all-purpose flour
1 teaspoon mustard powder
Cayenne pepper to taste or hot sauce such as Tapatio (optional)
12 oz. evaporated milk
1 ½ cups grated yellow cheddar cheese (mild is most universal, but medium, sharp or smoked can add a depth of flavor)
¼ cubed processed cheese
6 ounces Andouille sausage
1/3 cup red bell pepper, diced
1/3 cup green bell pepper diced
1/3 cup white onion, diced
1 teaspoon of all-purpose floor
1 teaspoon Cajun Seasoning (Recipe below)
Salt and pepper to taste

Directions
Dice and brown Andouille sausage with peppers and onion in skillet

Bring salted water to a boil.
Add pasta and cook until al dente.
Reserve 1 cup of pasta liquid for sauce.
Drain pasta.

In the saucepan, melt butter. Over medium heat, whisk in flour, mustard powder, and cayenne or hot sauce. Whisk for 1 minute before slowly incorporating evaporated milk and whisk to thoroughly mix. Lower heat to a simmer and whisk intermittently for about 5 minutes as sauce begins to thicken. Stir in both cheeses.

Add flour and Cajun Seasoning plus reserved pasta liquid to further thicken the sauce.
Stir in the meat, peppers, and onions.

Plate the mac and cheese. Season with salt and pepper to taste.

Cajun Seasoning

Makes 6 tablespoons
2 tablespoons salt
1 tablespoon paprika
1 tablespoon dried oregano
1 tablespoon black pepper
1 tablespoon oregano

Couch-Gating Mac and Cheese

Beers and brats go hand and hand with football. Try this twist on the classic tailgating combination the next time you are cheering on your favorite team. You're destined to score an extra point every time you serve this fan favorite. (Note: You can skip the beer if you are serving around children and still have a delish dish.)

Ingredients and Supplies
Pot of salted boiling water (Kosher salt works best)
Medium saucepan
Large (2 quart) baking dish

8 ounces of pasta (Elbows or Fusilli)
Non-stick cooking spray (or additional tablespoon of butter)
1 tablespoon of unsalted butter
1 tablespoon all-purpose flour
1 teaspoon mustard powder
Cayenne pepper to taste or hot sauce such as Tapatio (optional)
12 oz. evaporated milk
2 cups grated yellow cheddar cheese (medium or sharp)
¼ cubed processed cheese
8 ounces Bratwurst, cooked and diced
¼ cup of dark beer
2 tablespoons spicy brown mustard
Salt and pepper to taste

Directions
Preheat oven to 400 degrees.

Bring salted water to a boil.
Add pasta and cook until al dente.
Reserve 1 cup of pasta liquid for sauce.
Drain pasta.

In the saucepan, melt butter. Over medium heat, whisk in flour, mustard powder, and cayenne or hot sauce. Add beer and continue to whisk for 2 minutes.

Whisk for 1 minute before slowly incorporating evaporated milk and whisk to thoroughly mix. Lower heat to a simmer and whisk intermittently for about 5 minutes as sauce begins to thicken. Stir in 1 ½ cups of cheddar and all of the processed cheese.

Add all of the reserved pasta liquid, dark mustard, and brats. Mix through.

Coat baking dish, and transfer pasta. Top with the remaining cheddar cheese.
Bake for 15 minutes.

Cheeseburger Mac and Cheese

If beer and brats aren't your speed, this Cheeseburger Mac and Cheese works for both the couch-gating crowd as well as keeping the kids cheering.

Ingredients and Supplies
Pot of salted boiling water (Kosher salt works best)
Medium saucepan
Medium skillet
Large (2 quart) baking dish

8 ounces of pasta (Elbows or Fusilli)
1 tablespoon of unsalted butter
Non-stick cooking spray or additional tablespoon of butter
1 tablespoon all-purpose flour
1 teaspoon mustard powder
Cayenne pepper to taste or hot sauce such as Tapatio (optional)
12 oz. evaporated milk
2 cups grated yellow cheddar cheese (1/2 cup reserved for topping)
¼ cubed processed cheese
Salt and pepper to taste
½ lb. ground beef
¼ cup ketchup
¼ cup chopped dill pickles or relish
¼ cup, diced white onion

Directions

Brown beef in medium skillet and drain. Add ketchup, pickles/relish, and onions warm and mix ingredients together after removing skillet from heat. Set skillet aside.

Bring salted water to a boil.
Add pasta and cook until al dente.
Reserve 1 cup of pasta liquid for sauce.
Drain pasta.

In the saucepan, melt butter. Over medium heat, whisk in flour, mustard powder, and cayenne or hot sauce. Whisk for 1 minute before slowly incorporating evaporated milk and whisk to thoroughly mix. Lower heat to a simmer and whisk intermittently for about 5 minutes as sauce begins to thicken. Stir in both cheeses. Add all of the reserved pasta liquid.

Coat the baking dish. Pour and level half of the pasta mixture into the baking dish. Add in the meat mixture over the pasta. Add the remaining pasta mixture as a third layer. Top with remaining cheddar cheese.

Bake for 15 minutes.

Chili Cheese Mac

This mac and cheese is a nod to the popularity of chili cheese fries, minus the fries. Instead, tortilla or corn chips give this dish an added crunch. This is a great way to use leftover chili. If you don't have leftovers, canned chili can be used in its place.

Ingredients and Supplies
Pot of salted boiling water (Kosher salt works best)
Medium saucepan
Large (2 quart) baking dish

8 ounces of pasta (Elbows or Fusilli)
1 tablespoon of unsalted butter
Non-stick cooking spray or additional tablespoon of butter
1 tablespoon all-purpose flour
1 teaspoon mustard powder
Cayenne pepper to taste or hot sauce such as Tapatio (optional)
12 oz. evaporated milk
1 ½ cups grated yellow cheddar cheese (mild is most universal, but medium, sharp or smoked can add a depth of flavor)
¼ cubed processed cheese
1 ½ cups chili
¼ cup pepper jack cheese
½ cup crushed tortilla or corn chips

Directions
Preheat oven to 400 degrees
Bring salted water to a boil.

Add pasta and cook until al dente.
Reserve 1 cup of pasta liquid for sauce.
Drain pasta.

In the saucepan, melt butter. Over medium heat, whisk in flour, mustard powder, and cayenne or hot sauce. Whisk for 1 minute before slowly incorporating evaporated milk and whisk to thoroughly mix. Lower heat to a simmer and whisk intermittently for about 5 minutes as sauce begins to thicken. Stir in both cheeses. Add enough reserved pasta liquid to further thicken the sauce.

Coat the baking dish. Pour pasta mixture into the baking dish. Layer the chili evenly over the pasta. Top with pepper jack cheese and crushed chips.
Bake for 15 minutes.

10 Top Thick and Creamy Custard-Style Mac and Cheese Options

If you prefer the richer version of mac and cheese that works best with pasta shells, this final set of mac and cheese options is just the ticket for you. Recipes include kid-focused options as well as adult-friendly dishes, so there is something for everyone.

Tuna Veggie Mac and Cheese

Combine tuna and veggies to make a well-rounded and satisfying mac and cheese that takes the goodness of the popular fish and includes veggies, cheese and pasta to hit a home run that covers all the bases.

Ingredients and Supplies
Pot of salted boiling water (Kosher salt works best)
Large saucepan

8 ounces of pasta (shells or other small pasta)
½ teaspoon salt
3 tablespoons unsalted butter
2 large eggs
1 cup evaporated milk
3 cups shredded yellow cheddar cheese (Mild is the most universal but medium, sharp, or smoked can be incorporated for a deeper flavor profile)
Pinch of cayenne pepper (optional)
1 6 oz. can of tuna, drained
1 ½ cups of frozen peas and carrots, thawed

Directions
Bring salted water to a boil.
Add pasta and cook until al dente.
Reserve 1 cup of pasta liquid for sauce.
Drain pasta.
Toss in butter until melted and coating pasta.

In large saucepan over medium heat, whisk eggs, evaporated milk, salt, cheese, and cayenne pepper together. Continue to whisk until the mixture thickens (approximately 3 minutes). Add pasta and continue to stir and cook for another 2-3 minutes. Add reserved pasta liquid to thicken the sauce while stirring.

Stir in tuna and vegetables.

Plate and season with additional salt and pepper to taste.

Kid Friendly Mac and Cheese

Whether you are making the more traditional kid fare with the popular hot dogs or chopped bologna to keep the youngsters happy or you want to experience an old friend in the form of mac and cheese, this dish can hit the spot for a quick fun dish. The recipe is designed to take everything up a notch but can be easily simplified for younger palates.

Ingredients and Supplies
Pot of salted boiling water (Kosher salt works best)
Large saucepan

8 ounces of pasta (shells or other small pasta)
½ teaspoon salt
3 tablespoons unsalted butter
2 large eggs
1 cup evaporated milk
3 cups shredded yellow cheddar cheese (Mild is the most universal but medium, sharp, or smoked can be incorporated for a deeper flavor profile)
Pinch of cayenne pepper (optional)
1 ½ cups of diced hotdogs or bologna fried in a skillet
1 tablespoon deli mustard

Directions
Bring salted water to a boil.
Add pasta and cook until al dente.
Reserve 1 cup of pasta liquid for sauce.
Drain pasta.
Toss in butter until melted and coating pasta.

In large saucepan over medium heat, whisk eggs, evaporated milk, salt, cheese, and cayenne pepper together. Continue to whisk until the mixture thickens (approximately 3 minutes). Add pasta and continue to stir and cook for another 2-3 minutes. Add reserved pasta liquid to thicken the sauce while stirring.

Stir in hot dogs or bologna and mustard.
Plate and season with additional salt and pepper to taste.

Spaghetti Meatball Mac and Cheese

Whether you make your own meatballs or use frozen, premade ones from the store, this dish delights those who don't want the typical spaghetti and meatballs.

Ingredients and Supplies
Pot of salted boiling water (Kosher salt works best)
Large saucepan

8 ounces of pasta (shells or other small pasta)
½ teaspoon salt
3 tablespoons unsalted butter
2 large eggs
1 cup evaporated milk
3 cups shredded yellow cheddar cheese (Mild is the most universal but medium, sharp, or smoked can be incorporated for a deeper flavor profile)
Pinch of cayenne pepper (optional)
½ cup of spaghetti sauce
2 cups of meatballs, cooked (whole or diced)
2 tablespoons of grated Parmesan cheese

Directions
Bring salted water to a boil.
Add pasta and cook until al dente.
Reserve 1 cup of pasta liquid for sauce.
Drain pasta.
Toss in butter until melted and coating pasta.

In large saucepan over medium heat, whisk eggs, evaporated milk, salt, cheese, and cayenne pepper together. Continue to whisk until the mixture thickens (approximately 3 minutes). Add pasta and continue to stir and cook for another 2-3 minutes.

Add ¼ cup spaghetti sauce and mix thoroughly before adding reserved pasta liquid to thicken the sauce while stirring.

Stir in the meatballs until covered.
Plate and drizzle remaining spaghetti sauce over the top. Sprinkle with Parmesan cheese.

Mac and Cheese Carbonara

This nod to pasta Carbonara, another pasta dish that serves as comfort food, uses white cheddar instead of the yellow cheddar noted in the Thick Mac and Cheese recipe.

Ingredients and Supplies
Pot of salted boiling water (Kosher salt works best)
Large saucepan

8 ounces of pasta (shells or other small pasta)
½ teaspoon salt
3 tablespoons unsalted butter
2 large eggs
1 cup evaporated milk
3 cups shredded white cheddar cheese
1 cup canned sweet peas, drained
1 cup chopped ham

Directions
Bring salted water to a boil.
Add pasta and cook until al dente.
Reserve 1 cup of pasta liquid for sauce.
Drain pasta.
Toss in butter until melted and coating pasta.

In large saucepan over medium heat, whisk eggs, evaporated milk, salt, and cheese together. Continue to whisk until the mixture thickens (approximately 3 minutes). Add pasta and continue to stir and cook for another 2-3 minutes. Add reserved pasta liquid to thicken the sauce while stirring.

Stir in ham and peas.

Plate and season with additional salt and pepper to taste.

Chicken Fajita Mac and Cheese

Have a fiesta with this fajita inspired mac and cheese dish that can be a meal (and party) unto itself.

Ingredients and Supplies
Pot of salted boiling water (Kosher salt works best)
Large saucepan
Medium skillet

8 ounces of pasta (shells or other small pasta)
½ teaspoon salt
3 tablespoons unsalted butter
2 large eggs
1 cup evaporated milk
3 cups shredded yellow cheddar cheese (Mild is the most universal but medium, sharp, or smoked can be incorporated for a deeper flavor profile)
Pinch of cayenne pepper (optional)
½ lb. of chicken breast, cooked and sliced
Salt and pepper
1 medium yellow onion, sliced
1 green bell pepper, sliced
1 red bell pepper, sliced
1 clove garlic, diced
2 tablespoons of olive oil

Directions
Bring salted water to a boil.
Add pasta and cook until al dente.

While pasta is cooking, sauté the onions and the peppers in olive oil. Add garlic and chicken to coat. Season with salt and pepper.

Reserve 1 cup of pasta liquid for sauce.
Drain pasta.
Toss in butter until melted and coating pasta.

In large saucepan over medium heat, whisk eggs, evaporated milk, salt, cheese, and cayenne pepper together. Continue to whisk until the mixture thickens (approximately 3 minutes). Add pasta and continue to stir and cook for another 2-3 minutes. Add reserved pasta liquid to thicken the sauce while stirring.

Plate pasta as the base with the chicken and vegetables on top.

Philly Cheesesteak Mac and Cheese

Hello Philly! This mac and cheese is an ode to the classic sandwich for which the City of Brotherly is known. This dish is definitely a meal in itself. (Note: part of the cheddar in the recipe is replaced with Provolone cheese.)

Ingredients and Supplies
Pot of salted boiling water (Kosher salt works best)
Large saucepan
Medium skillet

8 ounces of pasta (shells or other small pasta)
½ teaspoon salt
3 tablespoons unsalted butter
2 large eggs
1 cup evaporated milk
2 cups shredded yellow cheddar cheese
1 cup Provolone cheese, diced
Pinch of cayenne pepper (optional)
½ of shredded beef or sliced "Steak Um", cooked
1 medium white onion, sliced
1 green bell pepper, sliced
1 red bell pepper, sliced
2 tablespoons of olive oil

Directions
Bring salted water to a boil.
Add pasta and cook until al dente.

Sauté onions and peppers in olive oil over high heat in a skillet. Remove from heat. Add meat to skillet to keep mixture warm while pasta is made.

Reserve 1 cup of pasta liquid for sauce.
Drain pasta.
Toss in butter until melted and coating pasta.

In large saucepan over medium heat, whisk eggs, evaporated milk, salt, cheese, and cayenne pepper together. Continue to whisk until the mixture thickens (approximately 3 minutes). Add pasta and continue to stir and cook for another 2-3 minutes. Add reserved pasta liquid to thicken the sauce while stirring.

Plate with mac and cheese as the base. Spoon the meat and vegetables over the pasta. Season with additional salt and pepper to taste.

Chorizo Queso Mac

Queso, which is Spanish for cheese, is a popular and hearty appetizer in many restaurants. This version of mac and cheese can serve as a kicked up starter or as a dish all by itself.

Ingredients and Supplies
Pot of salted boiling water (Kosher salt works best)
Large saucepan

8 ounces of pasta (shells or other small pasta)
½ teaspoon salt
3 tablespoons unsalted butter
2 large eggs
1 cup evaporated milk
2 cups shredded yellow cheddar cheese
4 ounces cream cheese, softened
Pinch of cayenne pepper (optional)
2 cups chorizo, cooked and drained
2/3 cup of red salsa
½ cup crushed tortilla or corn chips

Directions
Bring salted water to a boil.
Add pasta and cook until al dente.
Reserve 1 cup of pasta liquid for sauce.
Drain pasta.
Toss in butter until melted and coating pasta.

In large saucepan over medium heat, whisk eggs, evaporated milk, salt, cheddar cheese, cream cheese, and cayenne pepper together. Continue to whisk until the mixture thickens (approximately 3 minutes). Add pasta and continue to stir and cook for another 2-3 minutes. Add reserved pasta liquid to thicken the sauce while stirring.

Stir in chorizo and salsa.
Plate and top with crushed tortilla or corn chips.

Heartland Ham and Corn Mac

This combination of ham and corn is a nod to both hearty heartland favorites and the concept of traditional American comfort food. There's no way you can go wrong with this mix of food staples.

Ingredients and Supplies
Pot of salted boiling water (Kosher salt works best)
Large saucepan

8 ounces of pasta (shells or other small pasta)
½ teaspoon salt
3 tablespoons unsalted butter
2 large eggs
1 cup evaporated milk
2 cups shredded yellow cheddar cheese
4 ounces cream cheese, softened
Pinch of cayenne pepper (optional)
1 can creamed corn
2 cups of diced ham
1 bunch of scallions, chopped

Directions
Bring salted water to a boil.
Add pasta and cook until al dente.
Reserve 1 cup of pasta liquid for sauce.
Drain pasta.
Toss in butter until melted and coating pasta.

In large saucepan over medium heat, whisk eggs, evaporated milk, salt, cheddar cheese, cream cheese, and cayenne pepper together. Continue to whisk until the mixture thickens (approximately 3 minutes).

Add pasta and continue to stir and cook for another 2-3 minutes. Add reserved pasta liquid to thicken the sauce while stirring.

Stir in the can of creamed corn and add ham. Plate and top with scallions.

Southern Greens Mac and Cheese

Combine two soul food favorites in a single dish with collard greens and mac and cheese. Though the recipe is set up for collard greens they can easily be replaced with cooked spinach, kale, or a combination of other greens.

Ingredients and Supplies
Pot of salted boiling water (Kosher salt works best)
Large saucepan

8 ounces of pasta (shells or other small pasta)
½ teaspoon salt
3 tablespoons unsalted butter
2 large eggs
1 cup evaporated milk
3 cups shredded yellow cheddar cheese (Mild is the most universal but medium, sharp, or smoked can be incorporated for a deeper flavor profile)
Pinch of cayenne pepper (optional)
2 cups collard greens, cooked (or other desired cooked greens)
Hot sauce such as Tabasco or Tapatio
Fried onions or club crackers for topping

Directions
Bring salted water to a boil.
Add pasta and cook until al dente.
Reserve 1 cup of pasta liquid for sauce.
Drain pasta.
Toss in butter until melted and coating pasta.

In large saucepan over medium heat, whisk eggs, evaporated milk, salt, cheese, and cayenne pepper together. Continue to whisk until the mixture thickens (approximately 3 minutes). Add pasta and continue to stir and cook for another 2-3 minutes. Add reserved pasta liquid to thicken the sauce while stirring.

Stir in greens and add hot sauce to taste
Plate and top with fried onions or crushed club crackers.

Curried Chicken Mac and Cheese

East meets west in this aromatic and flavorful version of an American classic. The unlikely ingredients combine to make it feel like you are traveling the world through your taste buds.

Ingredients and Supplies
Pot of salted boiling water (Kosher salt works
    best)
Large saucepan

8 ounces of pasta (shells or other small pasta)
½ teaspoon salt
3 tablespoons unsalted butter
2 large eggs
1 cup evaporated milk
3 cups shredded yellow cheddar cheese
Pinch of cayenne pepper (optional)
2 cups cooked chicken, shredded
2 cups baby spinach, chopped
2 tablespoons tomato paste
1 tablespoon curry powder
½ cup unsweetened coconut milk

Directions
Bring salted water to a boil.
Add pasta and cook until al dente.
Reserve 1/2 cup of pasta liquid for sauce.
Drain pasta.
Toss in butter until melted and coating pasta.

In large saucepan over medium heat, whisk eggs, evaporated milk, salt, cheese, and cayenne pepper together. Continue to whisk until the mixture thickens (approximately 3 minutes). Add pasta and continue to stir and cook for another 2 minutes.

Add coconut milk, tomato paste, and curry. Use reserved pasta liquid to thicken the sauce while stirring. Place spinach in pasta and allow it to cook down. Add chicken and make sure everything is incorporated together.

Plate and season with additional salt and pepper to taste.

Conclusion

There you have it…more than a month's worth of mac and cheese goodness to suit the tastes of even the pickiest of eaters. Whether you keep it simple with just the basic recipes or make it a gourmet delight with ingredients like truffles and lobster, you can enjoy mac and cheese at any time and for any occasion.

I hope you have found some old favorites and well as new delights to try. These recipes can be tailored to your specific tastes by including additional ingredients that you enjoy. Once you master the basic recipes, it is easy to modify the selections. Part of the fun of mac and cheese is that it is easy and relatively inexpensive to experiment with, so have some fun of your own. If you find a new way to make mac and cheese, I'd love to hear about it. You can find me on Twitter via @GLYummies.

Don't forget…if you haven't already gotten the free mac and cheese recipes download as my personal thank you for purchasing this book, please visit:

www.synchron8publishing.com/GLMacandCheese

Thanks again, and happy eats and drinks to all!

About Synchron8 Publishing

Gina Lynn is one of the writers associated with Synchron8 Publishing. We are part micro-publisher and part author- collective, supporting those who have a passion for the written word in its various forms. Our authors work together to create of their own as well as help promote works of others. Writers benefit from Synchron8 Publishing resources whether they decide to self-publish or to go a more conventional publishing route.

We continue to expand and grow with new titles regularly announced. Our fiction line is launching a Flash Fiction contest in early 2015. Prizes include publishing opportunities for both a group anthology as well as a potential publishing contract to be the feature author in upcoming books in our Flash 40 and Flash 14 series.

Our catalogue includes: cookbooks, informational books, non-fiction, and various types of fiction.

Learn more at **www.synchron8publishing.com**

www.ingramcontent.com/pod-product-compliance
Lightning Source LLC
Chambersburg PA
CBHW071612040426
42452CB00008B/1323